# Ways to....

# CHANGE *it!*

**Henry Pluckrose**

Photography by Chris Fairclough

**FRANKLIN WATTS**

London • New York • Sydney • Toronto

What do we mean by change? Which one of these things...

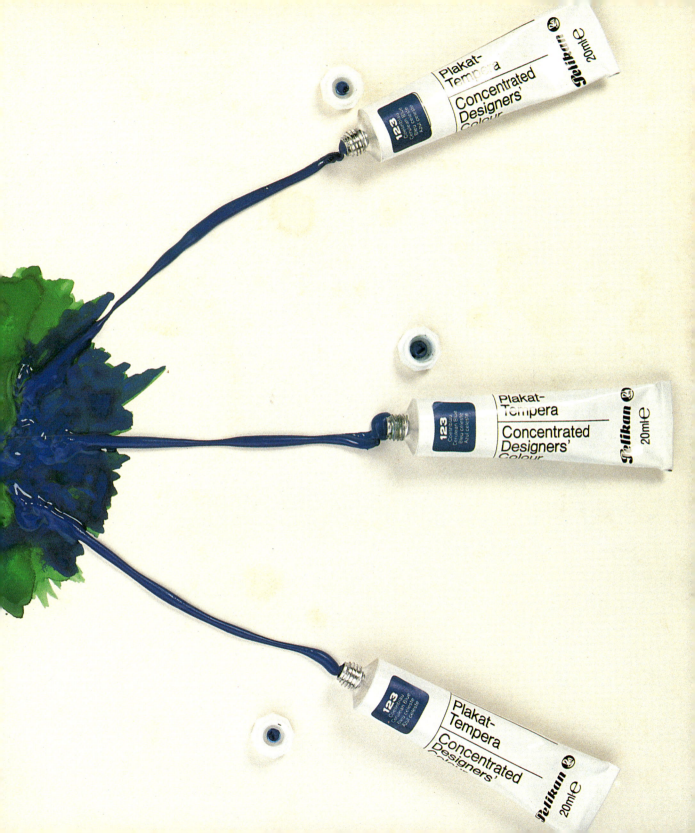

Franklin Watts
96 Leonard Street
London EC2A 4RH

Franklin Watts Australia
14 Mars Road
Lane Cove
NSW 2066

UK ISBN: 0 7496 0161 2

A CIP catalogue record for this book
is available from the British Library.

Editor: Kate Petty
Design: K & Co
Artwork: Aziz Khan

Typeset in England
by Lineage, Watford
Printed in Italy by
G. Canale S.p.A., Turin

has been used to make each of these?

**How are things changed?**

**To make a cake we mix the ingredients together.**

The mixture is baked in a hot oven.

The heat turns the raw mixture into a cake.

**Jelly is made with boiling water. It sets into a shape as it cools.**

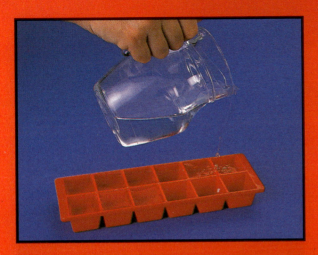

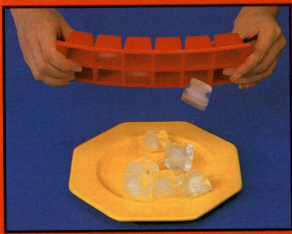

Water changes to ice when it gets very cold. How do you melt ice?

Water can change dry powder into a liquid.

Which is easier to paint with?

**What change is there when yellow and blue are mixed together?**

**Some things change their shape. A bag looks different when filled with groceries.**

Balloons change
shape when filled
with air.

Clothes can look
a different
shape…

...with people
inside them...

**Some things change as they grow.
Can you match these pictures?**

eggs

acorn

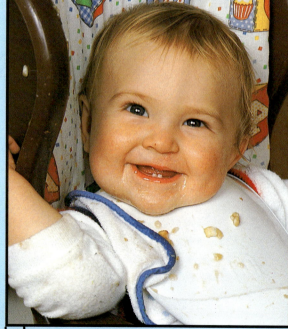

baby

bulb

**daffodils**

**old person**

**oak tree**

**duck**

We need tools to change trees like this...

into wooden
furniture or
wooden toys.

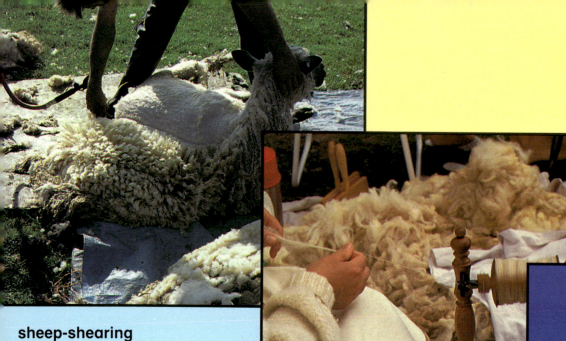

sheep-shearing

spinning

dyeing

Many things are done to change wool from sheep into clothes. The sheep has to be sheared and the wool…

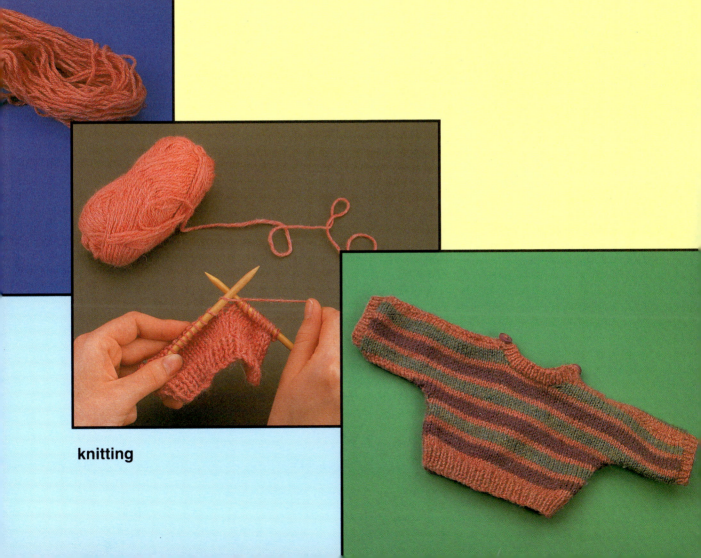

...spun,
...dyed,
and knitted
into the
right shape.

knitting

**Most of these machines help cooks to turn raw ingredients into something to eat or drink.**

**Which is the odd one out?**

**There are many ways in which things change. Can you match these pictures?**

dough

eggs

summer

milk

winter

cheese

bread

toad

# Things to do

## ● Changing colours

Put a wet blob of yellow paint on a piece of paper. Mix some blue paint into it. What happens?

Put a wet blob of red paint on a piece of paper. Mix some yellow paint into it. What happens?

What new colours are made if you mix
— black and white?

— red and blue?

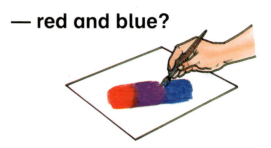

— yellow with red and then with blue?

## ● Looking through a colour

Find some coloured cellophane (sweet wrappers will do well).
Close one eye and look through a piece of red cellophane. What do you notice?

Find some other colours to look through – green, yellow or blue. What changes are there in the colours of the things you are looking at?

## ● How many times a day do you

— change your shoes?
— change your clothes?
— change your seat?

## ● Changing a flat shape

Cut a piece of paper into four pieces, like this

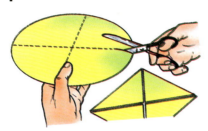

or this

Now rearrange the pieces to make different patterns. How many different patterns can you make?

## ● Changing a solid shape

Find a piece of modelling clay. Can you shape it into ...?

| | |
|---|---|
| a ball | a worm |
| a bridge | a face |
| a brick | a plate |
| a house | a bath |

## ● What do we mean by...?

Changing hands
Changing money
Changing places
Changing sides
Changing trains
A change of heart
A change in the weather

## Words about changing

| | |
|---|---|
| alter | improve |
| become | make |
| bend | melt |
| camouflage | mould |
| colour | rearrange |
| decay | repair |
| decrease | reshape |
| develop | shift |
| dye | turn |
| grow | twist |